The Way of Pilgrimage is like a new best friend! You can walk right into its welcoming presence and begin at once to find fresh truths sprouting up from ancient sources. It will become a trusted guide for those who accompany youth and young adults on their paths of meaning-making.

It promises especially satisfying moments for leaders who wish to engage others in the rhythmic paces of spiritual formation. The weekly gatherings show us how to move from deeply ingrained habits of content-based Bible study into soul-tending practices of contemplation and community that open us to transformation.

—THE REVEREND DR. DORI BAKER
Author, *Doing Girlfriend Theology: God-Talk with Young Women*
United Methodist pastor and professor of youth ministry and Christian education

As an organization completely dedicated to the art of pilgrimage, we are overjoyed with *The Way of Pilgrimage* resources. *The Way of Pilgrimage* is a comprehensive and passionate guide that brings us back to our ancient heritage of pilgrimage through modern eyes and practical application.

Utilize these resources to teach your youth God's unique design of our lives as journeys of exploration and adventure. There is no better resource available to date that prepares your teens as lifelong pilgrims.

—SHAWN SMALL
Executive director, Wonder Voyage Pilgrimages

Finally—a spiritual resource for youth and young adults with depth and meaning! Upper Room Books continues its Companions in Christ series with an insightful and creative journey for Generation Next. I love this resource!

—BO PROSSER
Coordinator for congregational life, Cooperative Baptist Fellowship

This inspiring resource meets participants wherever they are in their spiritual walk and gently moves them toward a deeper understanding of their own pilgrimage. In the context of a Christian community of travelers, participants shed light on the most unexamined corners of their souls. . . .

As an educator of secondary students, I greatly appreciate how consistently this text works to provide spiritual development activities for every kind of learner—from still meditation to verbal expression to artistic interpretations.

—JESSICA ROSENTHAL
United Methodist educator and youth helper

The Way of Pilgrimage is a wonderful doorway into the spiritual life. Like the bountiful feast that God sets before us, these volumes are full of wisdom and blessing. Those who accept the challenge to walk with Christ will benefit greatly from this guide. Its exercises are both simple and rich. At every point, the members of the group are encouraged to journey into the heart of God.

—THE REVEREND DANIEL WOLPERT
Pastor, First Presbyterian Church, Crookston, Minn.
Codirector, Minnesota Institute of Contemplation and Healing (MICAH)
Author, *Leading a Life with God*

THE BIBLE: PILGRIMAGE TRAVEL GUIDE

PARTICIPANT'S BOOK

Ciona Rouse

VOLUME **2**

UPPER ROOM BOOKS®
NASHVILLE

THE BIBLE: PILGRIMAGE TRAVEL GUIDE
Participant's Book Volume 2
Copyright © 2007 by Upper Room Books®.
All rights reserved.
The Upper Room® Web site http://www.upperroom.org

At the time of publication all Web sites referenced in this book were valid. However, due to the fluid nature of the Internet some addresses may have changed or the content may no longer be relevant.

Cover design: Left Coast Design, Portland, OR
Interior design: Gore Studio, Inc., Nashville, TN
Typesetting: PerfecType, Nashville, TN
First printing: 2007

ISBN-13:   978-0-8358-9835-5
ISBN-10:   0-8358-9835-0

LIBRARY OF CONGRESS CATALOG IN PUBLICATION DATA
Rouse, Ciona.
  The Bible : pilgrimage travel guide : participant's book / Ciona Rouse.
      p. cm.— (The way of pilgrimage ; v. 2)
  Includes bibliographical references (p. 72)
  1. Christian youth—Religious life. 2. Bible—Devotional use. 3.
Spiritual formation. I. Rouse, Ciona. Way of pilgrimage. II. Title.
  BV4531.3.R68 2007
   263'.041—dc22

                                                    2007003689

Printed in the United States of America

CONTENTS

MEET THE WRITER

Ciona Rouse lives in Nashville, Tennessee, and is a freelance writer for a number of United Methodist publications and groups. Formerly a director of the The United Methodist Church's Shared Mission Focus on Young People, Ciona attends Belmont United Methodist Church and volunteers with the youth there. She enjoys music, movies, and Middle Eastern dance.

ACKNOWLEDGMENTS

The Way of Pilgrimage is a new adventure in spiritual formation for a new generation of Companions in Christ groups. The original twenty-eight-week *Companions in Christ* resource was published by Upper Room Books in spring 2001. The ensuing Companions in Christ series has been designed to create settings in which people can respond to God's call to an ever-deepening communion and wholeness in Christ—as individuals, as members of a small group, and as part of a congregation. Building upon the Companions in Christ foundational vision, *The Way of Pilgrimage* is written for a younger audience of senior high youth and college freshmen.

The first consultation for developing *The Way of Pilgrimage* took place in Nashville in February 2005. We are deeply grateful to these consultants and to the writers of the Leader's Guide and Participant's Books: Sally Chambers, Kyle Dugan, Steve Matthews, Craig Mitchell, Jeremy Myers, Jonathon Norman, Kara Lassen Oliver, Gavin Richardson, Ciona Rouse, Jessica Rosenthal, Daniel Wolpert, and Jenny Youngman. Special thanks to Stephen Bryant, visionary leader of the Companions in Christ resources and publisher of Upper Room Ministries. All of the daily exercises found in this book were developed and written by him.

We are also indebted to those who reviewed the early manuscript and offered their insights on theology and pilgrimage: The Reverend Matthew Corkern, Christ Church Cathedral Episcopal Church in Nashville, Tennessee; Sally Chambers, St. Paul's Episcopal Church in Franklin, Tennessee; and Jeremy Myers, Augsburg College in Minneapolis, Minnesota.

The following churches and groups tested portions of early versions of *The Way of Pilgrimage*:

> Belmont United Methodist Church in Nashville, Tennessee (leader: Jessica Rosenthal)
>
> Wesley United Methodist Church in Coral Gables, Florida (leader: the Reverend Cesar J. Villafaña)

First United Methodist Church in Hendersonville, Tennessee (leader: Gavin Richardson)

North Park University in Chicago, Illinois (leaders: Susan Braun and Jodi DeYoung)

Milford United Methodist Church in Milford, Michigan (leader: Sherry Foster)

Westminster Presbyterian Church in Eugene, Oregon (leaders: Jen Butler and Katie Stocks)

St. Paul's Episcopal Church in Richmond, Virginia (leader: Steve Matthews)

SoulFeast 2006 Youth Program in Lake Junaluska, North Carolina (leader: Ciona Rouse)

The Companions in Christ Staff Team
Upper Room Ministries

INTRODUCTION

You have made us for yourself, O Lord,
and our heart is restless till it rests in you.

—Saint Augustine

We are a pilgrim people, always moving, always wanting more, never satisfied, never full and never finished. We are a pilgrim people.

Throughout the scriptures, God continually reminds us of our pilgrim hearts and calls us back to the path that leads us home. The psalmist declares, "For I am . . . a traveler passing through, as my ancestors were before me" (Psalm 39:12, NLT). And the letter to the Hebrews says it quite simply, We are "strangers and pilgrims on the earth" (11:13, NKJV). The word *pilgrim* comes from the Latin word meaning "resident alien." This world is not our home. Our life here on earth is just one stop on this all-encompassing pilgrimage, a physical and spiritual journey home to the One to whom we truly belong. We *are* a pilgrim people.

The travel guide for the pilgrim is the Bible. Through the scriptures we hear the story of God's people, learn from pilgrims who have gone before us, receive the rules for the road, find purpose in our journey, and discover the hope that waits for us. But beyond these gifts, through scripture we hear most clearly the words God has for us on our pilgrimage. Listening for God's voice is an essential practice for a pilgrim; only when we first listen can we follow where God leads. No matter which book in the Bible we open, what chapter and verse we read, we find God there. The Bible becomes a meeting place, holy ground where pilgrims and God converge and converse. So scripture becomes not only the guide for our pilgrimage but the place where we find and hear the One we seek.

Before we begin, here are a few rules for the road:

There is a difference between being a tourist and being a pilgrim.

Just as we can travel to holy places as a tourist, not fully engaged or fully present, we also can walk this spiritual pilgrimage of faith as a tourist.

Tourists may take snapshots of places along the way and yet still keep their hearts far removed, offering empty words to those they meet. Tourists also may be here only for the community and not the journey. *This is a journey for pilgrims.*

The travel guide for the pilgrim is the Bible. Through the scriptures we hear the story of God's people, learn from those pilgrims who have gone before us, receive the rules for the road, find purpose in our journey, and discover the hope that waits for us. But beyond these gifts, through scripture we hear most clearly the words God has for us on our pilgrimage. Listening for God's voice is one of the most essential practices of a pilgrim, for only then can we follow where God leads. In the Bible, our travel guide, no matter what book we open to, what chapter and verse we read, we find God there. The Bible is a meeting place, holy ground where pilgrims and God converge and converse. So scripture becomes not only the guide for our pilgrimage but the place where we find and hear the One whom we seek.

Companions along the way are essential to pilgrimage.

Keep in mind that even though we travel with others, each pilgrim must make his or her own journey. As fellow pilgrims we journey side by side, looking out together for the One we seek.

Each weekly gathering is a stop along the way.

Each gathering is space carved out and made holy. When we gather together, the gate between God and us seems wider, and the intersection of heaven and earth more apparent. Each gathering is a place that says, *Welcome, pilgrims. Welcome to this respite. Welcome to this holy place.*

Rhythm is part of our daily routine as pilgrims.

In medieval times, pilgrims would set out on their journey in exactly the same way. Ritual and repetition were intrinsic to pilgrimage. And because pilgrims followed the same path, we can follow medieval pilgrim trails today in Europe and in the Holy Land. Every Good Friday pilgrims walk the way of the cross, the same path Jesus walked to his death (according to tradition). The repetition and rhythm of the daily exercises and readings are essential to this participant's book. So stick with them, and you will find that particular prayers, scriptures, and practices that are repeated through our journey will begin to sink from your head down to your heart; they will become as familiar and comforting as wearing a favorite old pair of shoes.

Pilgrimage is about being present in the present.

This pilgrimage is about waking up and paying attention to our lives. It also involves remembering our past. As we live our days awake to God in prayer, we will become present to God and to life.

This is a journey of the heart as well as the head.

In this journey, prayer, conversation, listening, reading, noticing, and looking are transformed from activities of the mind to practices of the heart.

You are invited to engage in the exercises each day and read the daily readings. The shaded paragraphs you'll see in the readings contain an essential idea in the passage. Be sure to get yourself a journal to use for exercises, reflections, and group meetings.

So welcome, pilgrim! May you journey faithfully and with integrity. May you make great strides, though this pilgrimage does not literally go far. As you learn to listen for the word of God, allowing it to guide you on this way, may you come to know who you really are and what you truly seek. And may Christ "dwell in your hearts through faith, as you are being rooted and grounded in love. . . . May [you] have the power to comprehend, with all the saints, what is the breadth and length and height and depth, and to know the love of Christ that surpasses knowledge, so that you may be filled with all the fullness of God" (Eph. 3:17-19).

Welcome home. Welcome to *The Way of Pilgrimage*.

—Sally Chambers
Coauthor, *The Way of Pilgrimage* Leader's Guide

A WORD ABOUT THE WEEK

The travel guide for Christian pilgrims is the Bible. Through the scriptures we hear the story of God's people; we learn from those pilgrims who have gone before us; we receive the rules for the road, find purpose in our journey, and discover the hope that waits for us. Each day, to prepare for the daily exercises, take a moment to quiet yourself and open your heart to the guidance of the Holy Spirit. It is helpful to set aside a particular place for prayer and meditation. Allow yourself ten to fifteen minutes of quiet for each daily exercise. Keep a journal or blank notebook beside you to record your thoughts, questions, prayers, and images.

THE ILLUMINATING WORD OF GOD

Day 1 Exercise

READ PSALM 119:97-105.

> *Oh, how I love your law! It is my meditation all day long. . . .*
> *Your word is a lamp to my feet and a light to my path.*
> —Psalm 119:97, 105

REFLECT What parts of the Bible already live in you and serve as a travel guide, "a lamp to my feet and a light to my path"? What is your favorite Bible story or scripture passage? Reflect on why and how you came to cherish it. How has God spoken to you through it?

PRAY Hold your Bible. Feel its weight and sense the spiritual treasure it holds. Pray that God will be revealed to you in new ways this week through the scripture.

ACT Read a favorite passage from your Bible tonight by the light of a flashlight. If you can't think of a favorite, read Psalm 119:97-105 again. Cherish each word.

Day 1   Reading

As a child, I understood the Bible to be the Word of God. I imagined God hanging out on the clouds holding a pen and a pad, drafting the big book. Later in life I imagined the biblical writers sitting down with their pens as God dictated word-for-word what they should say. But there are too many styles, different ways of telling the same story, and somewhat contradictory statements in the Bible for that to be true. I could not imagine that would be the case if God relayed the story to the writers word-for-word.

Over time and through study I have learned that the formation of the Bible happened in stages. Stage one was simple storytelling. Parents told their children the story of the Hebrew people leaving Egypt and of Jesus' ministry, death, and resurrection. In stage two these stories were written down by several individuals, editors, and revisers. Stage three entailed copying and sharing these manuscripts. Before printing presses existed, these stories were copied by hand and read aloud in worship settings.

During stage four certain writings gained authority in different places. For example, the church in Rome probably used Mark's Gospel, while Antioch used Matthew's. Stage five involved formation of collections and categories: the Law (the first five books), the Writings (the rest of the Hebrew scriptures), and the Gospels. In the final stage these collections were translated and circulated throughout the Roman Empire.

Now, informed by its history and formed by its message, I understand the Bible to be the living, breathing Word of God. Nearly every morning as I walk to my church for time alone with God, I ask the Spirit to speak through the reading of the Word.

When we approach scripture with the same faith and prayer as those who wrote the books of the Bible, the Spirit inspires our listening in the same way that the Spirit inspired the writers of scripture. When we listen to the Bible with an open heart, we create space for God to speak to us a fresh word of grace, a living word of guidance—here and now.

During the next six weeks we will explore the Bible as the travel guide for our pilgrimage. Through scripture we will hear the story of God's people, learn from pilgrims who have gone before us, receive rules for the road, find purpose in our journey, and discover the hope that awaits us.

STORIES INSPIRED BY GOD

Day 2 Exercise

READ PSALM 1.

Happy are those who . . . delight in the law of the LORD . . . they are like trees planted by streams of water.—Psalm 1:1, 3

REFLECT As a preface to the Psalter, this psalm conveys the promise of the Bible: those who study God's law (the law of life) and live by God's Word will be "like trees planted by streams of water" (Ps. 1:3).

Drawing on the imagery of the psalm, sketch a picture of two trees—one on each side of a page. Make one tree a picture of your life as it is. (Is it healthy or shriveled? Are its roots near or far from a stream?) With the second tree, depict your life as it could be.

Beneath and between the trees, list or write out words from any verses of scripture in which you have found streams of life, comfort, or strength.

PRAY Spend a few moments quietly opening your heart to what God may be saying to you.

ACT Each time you see a tree in the coming day, recall one of your favorite passages of scripture and feel the nourishment of God.

Day 2 Reading

When my sister and I were old enough to understand, my mom shared stories about her grandparents, her brothers and sisters, her high school friends, and Uncle Remus. Uncle Remus was a tall, wonderful old man who told the best stories. Mom told us how he whipped together fascinating tales about a cunning rabbit and a mean fox. She always told Uncle Remus stories with amazing energy.

I was well into elementary school before I realized that Uncle Remus was not a member of our family. In fact, Uncle Remus was a legendary storyteller created in a series of books by Joel Chandler Harris. But my mom knew these stories so well that they became her own, and she passed them to me so that they could also become mine.

The Bible includes a compilation of stories passed on from many generations ago to those of us who live today and those who will be here in years to come. The Bible is a library of stories and teachings to be told again and again, to know so well that they become our own.

The Bible holds stories of adventure, of deceit, of kings and queens, of conversions and miracles. We find first-person accounts of Jesus, visions from God, and ancient creation accounts among its stories. Most importantly, the Spirit of God inspires the Bible's stories (unlike the Uncle Remus stories, which are tall tales to entertain and teach children). The Bible weaves together many stories to tell the larger story of God's call to individuals and nations into a covenant relationship of love and truth.

Much like Jesus, the Bible combines humanity and divinity. The sixty-six books of the Bible were recorded by humans yet inspired by God. We read the stories of this book with our human eyes and minds, but we pray for divine wisdom to understand as we study the scripture. Through these very human words in human context we are able to hear God speak to us.

WEEK ONE THE LIVING, BREATHING WORD OF GOD

THE TESTAMENTS

Day 3   Exercise

READ GENESIS 1.

Then God said, "Let us make humankind in our image." . . . And it was so.—Genesis 1:26, 30

REFLECT The Old Testament begins with Genesis and the story of Creation. Again and again in this opening story, we read, "Then God said. . . . And it was so." In God, unlike us, word and action always correspond. What God speaks becomes reality—in God's own time.

Ponder the word and promise in Gen. 1:26-27 that "God created humankind in [God's] image." What parts of yourself bear little resemblance to God's image? What could happen if you opened your life wide to the same creative Word that spoke Creation into being? Imagine yourself as a perfectly completed creation and hear God saying, "And it was so."

PRAY What is God saying to you these days ("And God said . . .")? With a leap of faith, ask that God's will be done in you ("And it was so"). Then write what excites or scares you about that possibility.

ACT Take a risk this week. How can you reflect God's image in your own life?

Day 3 Reading

The Bible consists of two testaments, the "Old" and the "New." *Testament* simply means a covenant made between God and humankind.

Each testament tells of God's relationship with human beings as they struggle to fully recover and realize the image of God. The Old and New Testaments are inseparably linked to each other.

Let's talk a little about the OT (Old Testament)—the part of the Bible we sometimes think of as having laborious lists of laws, incredible drama, and no Jesus. Sometimes it's just easier to stick with the stories of Christ found in the NT (New Testament). But the OT is rich and wonderful. We also call the Old Testament the Hebrew scriptures because it was written originally in Hebrew and remains the Bible of the Jewish people, the scriptures Jesus himself read and followed. He lived these scriptures more fully than any other person. Through Jesus the Word of God truly became flesh and walked among us.

The NT tells us that Christ, being divine, was there at the beginning of Creation, at one with our Creator ("In the beginning was the Word, and the Word was with God, and the Word was God. He was in the beginning with God" [John 1:1]). Jesus, being also fully human, has a genealogy that traces from Abraham to King David down to Joseph and Mary (Matt. 1:1-17). His history is the history of the Hebrew scriptures. Jesus, the Word of God in person, has become the lens through which Christians read the OT.

Additionally, the OT sets forth God's plan to save the world through Jesus Christ. We hear God promise that Abraham's family line will be a blessing to all nations (Gen. 12:1-3). This promise is fulfilled through Jesus. The prophets of the Hebrew scriptures also foretell the coming of the Messiah (Isa. 7:10-16; 42:1-17).

Although Christianity began as a sect of Judaism, by the late first century the "child" had separated from the "parent." The existence of the New Testament raises an important question: How can it be understood without recognizing its integral connection to the Hebrew scriptures? The answer is, it cannot. The earliest Christians lived by the Hebrew scriptures just as Jesus and other Jews did. Consequently, the Jewish people can live out of the Hebrew scriptures as they have down through the centuries, but Christians cannot find their path using only the NT. They must hold the two testaments together.

A LITERARY SMORGASBORD

Day 4 Exercise

READ JOHN 1:1-18.

In the beginning was the Word. . . . He was in the beginning with God. . . . And the Word became flesh and lived among us, and we have seen his glory.—John 1:1-2, 14

REFLECT All four Gospels tell the story of Jesus, but each begins differently. John skips birth stories and starts with the remarkable claim that Jesus is God's Word spoken from the beginning of time into history, a Word that "became flesh and lived among us" as a person, Jesus Christ.

Think about what it means to speak of Jesus as "Word." In whom have you glimpsed a reflection of "the Word made flesh"? What message does that person's life communicate? Whom do you know who lives the gospel message in a way that makes the Bible come to life for you?

PRAY Pray that Jesus Christ, the Word of God, might become as real to you as your own flesh and bone. Pray to embody this Word in your own life.

ACT Imagine what it would look like to shine with God's glory in your life today. Express its beauty in every way you can think to do so.

Day 4 Reading

At a church retreat Sarah admitted to the group that the Bible bored her. She preferred reading and writing poetry, she said. Rather than reading the Bible to grow spiritually, she simply wrote prayers to God. What Sarah did not know was how many different literary forms are found in the Bible: poetry, prose, parables, prayers, history and wisdom literature.

For the poetry fan, nearly one-third of the Old Testament books include beautiful, lyrical poetry. Sarah's pastor encouraged her to look at the Psalms, Job, Song of Solomon, and Lamentations to learn more about how ancient authors wrote poetry and prayers to God.

Sarah was fascinated to think of the Bible as a library of many types of literature rather than one big, boring book. In this library, the bulk of the writing is prose. Sarah learned, however, that this prose covers a wide range of topics: danger, betrayal, murder, marriage, infidelity, royalty, laws, wars, miracles, doubt, faith, and more.

One particularly interesting genre is the parable—a short story in which common objects and situations are used to illustrate a lesson about God or reveal a truth. Jesus often spoke in parables (see Matt. 18:10-14; 21:33-41; Luke 11:5-13). Sarah realized that she could write her own parables.

Sarah also discovered that her prayers to God are based on a biblical tradition. Prayers are sprinkled throughout the Bible, especially in the Psalms and the Gospels. The New Testament letters also contain prayers.

Sarah learned the Bible has its equivalent of the History Channel. The history and biography books tell the story of God's people from the creation of humanity to the creation of the church. Some books are primarily historical (Joshua, 1 and 2 Kings, and Acts), while others deal with the laws and rules of God's people (especially the first five books).

Sarah's greatest discovery was the Wisdom Literature (mostly in Proverbs, Job, and Ecclesiastes). It contains snippets of wisdom, the kind of advice she received from her grandmother, but this advice came from God! Right there in the book of Proverbs Sarah found wise counsel on friendship, happiness, hardships, honesty, marriage, and life.

While at first Sarah found it difficult to stay engaged in reading some of these stories, she began to explore the full library of literature housed in this one book: the Bible.

WEEK ONE

THE LIVING, BREATHING WORD OF GOD

LETTERS FOR THE PILGRIMAGE

Day 5   Exercise

READ 2 CORINTHIANS 3:1-6.

You show that you are a letter of Christ, prepared by us, written not with ink but with the Spirit of the living God, not on tablets of stone but tablets of human hearts.—2 Corinthians 3:3

REFLECT What an affirmation we find in here! The apostle Paul commends his faith friends in Corinth with glowing words.

Think about your life as a letter you write with your actions and attitudes as well as your words. What does your "letter" this week say or not say about Christ and his life in you? What word from Christ would the Spirit like to write on the tablet of your heart for all to see and read?

PRAY In silence repeat the word God would write on your heart. Sit with this word, repeating it over and over, offering it as a prayer to God.

ACT To whom would God send you today as a letter of encouragement? Act on the answer.

Day 5 Reading

Dear Fellow Pilgrim,

Grace and peace to you! I hope that you are enjoying these explorations with your travel guide, the Bible, on your pilgrim journey.

E-mail is a wonderful creation, don't you think? No more checking the mailbox each day, hoping that the mail carrier delivered a letter for you! When I e-mail friends, they typically respond immediately. I must admit, though, that I sometimes miss getting snail mail.

I imagine the epistle (letter) writers of the Bible would have considered e-mail an incredible invention. From his prison cell in Rome, Paul could have typed a quick note to the Christians of Ephesus and received a speedy response from them. Instead, Paul had to write lengthy letters, hoping to share all he could with his fellow pilgrims in case he was harmed and unable to get to them.

Many of the biblical letters are written to individuals and to early church communities as a means of encouragement, accountability, and advice for Christian living. Paul speaks to specific struggles of the church at Corinth in his first letter to the Corinthians. He answers questions from new believers in his letters to the Thessalonians. In his first letter, Peter writes to the churches of Asia Minor, giving them advice for their pilgrimage.

On our pilgrimage, we will also encounter encouragement, accountability, and guidance through the biblical epistles. These letters draw from and illuminate the law, writings, and gospels that believers of old already studied and prayed. Although they are written to specific people at a specific time, we can also hear God speak to us through them now. Not every piece of advice for people of that day will fit our time. But when we work through the context of their situations, we learn that these letters offer good support and guidance for our journey.

So, maybe I'll put the computer aside every once in a while and journey back to the days of old. I'll pull out pen and paper and write my own epistles to fellow pilgrims on the way.

Sincerely,
Ciona

A WORD ABOUT THE WEEK

For Christians the Bible is a family photo album, full of memories and stories from our family history. By knowing our stories we get a better understanding of who we are and how we can live our lives more faithfully as God's pilgrim people. Give yourself the gift of a quiet space of fifteen minutes or so to reflect on scripture and pray. Keep your journal close by to note your thoughts and questions.

THE LEGACY OF ANCIENT PILGRIMS

Day 1 Exercise

READ GENESIS 28:10-22.

> *Then Jacob woke from his sleep and said, "Surely the LORD is in this place—and I did not know it!"—Genesis 28:16*

REFLECT This well-known story tells how God woke Jacob up from spiritual slumber to the divine presence and promise in his life. When have you been most like Jacob—spiritually asleep, unaware of divine presence or purpose in your life?

If you could travel back through your life with spiritual eyes opened, where would you marvel like Jacob, "Surely the LORD is in this place—and I did not know it!"? Close your eyes and take a mental tour of your life through early, middle, and recent years. As each memory comes to mind, prayerfully recite Jacob's exclamation. Jot down your remembrances and new awareness.

PRAY Express your gratitude to God for being with you more than you ever knew.

ACT Look for God today—in nature, the face of a friend, or your own actions—and give thanks.

Day 1 Reading

Our life's pilgrimage is long. Laced with failures and uncertainty at times, the way gets hard. I fall and have trouble getting up on my own. I make mistakes and struggle with how to make things right again. I doubt whether I am being faithful enough, if God will get me through yet another obstacle, or if I can continue the walk on this long road.

The pilgrimage is fruitful. Lined with tulips at times, the path of life shows hope. Some days I see the fruit my faithfulness bears. I feel God's presence surrounding me. I am inspired, encouraged, and excited. I believe that I will make it to the heart of God.

The pilgrimage is difficult, triumphant, stressful, victorious, tearful, hopeful, and filled with many surprises. But in all these experiences, one thing the pilgrimage should never be is lonely. Our journey continues the story of a long lineage of faithful people. Because our legacy goes back to the days of Creation, we travel with the saints and sinners of the biblical story. Our story is the story of God's people, so God's people of yesterday and today are our fellow pilgrims.

Our fellow pilgrims include those who recounted and wrote God's Word: kings, paupers, tax collectors, prophets, physicians, fishermen, prisoners, poets, and musicians. The story includes people just like us today: mothers, daughters, sons, fathers, betrayers, judges, adulterers, soldiers, thieves, and disciples.

Our fellow pilgrims encountered long, difficult stretches as well as fruitful, beautiful times on their pilgrimages. They were faithful and doubtful. They worshiped God and denied Christ. They each walked a special journey just as we each do. Even God, in the form of the Son, came to earth and walked the pilgrimage with us.

Their stories are the legacy on which we build. Together their accounts create a beautiful and informative travel guide.

THE JOURNAL OF OTHER PILGRIMS

Day 2   Exercise

READ EXODUS 17:1-7.

From the wilderness . . . the whole congregation of the Israelites journeyed by stages.—Exodus 17:1

REFLECT At some level, the Exodus story shapes all other Hebrew and Christian stories. This episode tells of the Israelites' faith struggles as they "journeyed by stages" from slavery in Egypt through the wilderness toward the Promised Land. As you reflect on this text, look for what brought the Hebrews through their wilderness.

Identify a stage in your journey when you were spiritually thirsty, discouraged, or empty. What happened? What brought you through your desert? Write your reflections.

PRAY Share your questions, wonderings, and gratitude with God. Listen for God's response.

ACT Each time you take a drink of water today, pause to remember that your journey is both physical and spiritual. Ask God to fill you and equip you for the journey.

Day 2 Reading

I own at least ten journals, several of which I wrote during my childhood. I write in four journals right now. One contains my poetry. Another holds my prayers. Another records my daily thoughts. And still another includes notes and ideas from my dance class.

When I was seven, I wrote notes in my diary to future readers. I left my legacy on those pages for whoever might find it. I assumed that a producer or publisher would read my journal one day and want to turn it into a television show like *Little House on the Prairie* or an award-winning book and movie like *The Diary of Anne Frank*.

The biblical authors definitely were not thinking of television or best sellers as they wrote their entries. In fact, they were not even thinking about being included in the biblical canon, what we now call the Holy Scriptures. But their writings provide a peek into their lives and faith—some recorded much like a diary.

For example, the book of Acts reveals the daily trials of early Christians. We learn of their persecution and the way the followers of Jesus faithfully shared God's word through it all.

In his letters, we get to know Paul. In his letter to the Romans, Paul gives instructions for interpreting the gospel. In his more personal letters to Timothy, we see how Paul interacts with this friend and fellow pilgrim.

We get a glimpse into the thoughts of King David and the other psalmists when we read the Psalms. We learn about times David cried out to God for help. We hear the psalmists' shouts of praise and thanksgiving and also their fears and frustrations. Reading the Psalms, Job, or Song of Solomon is almost like peering into your sister's diary because we discover the honest and intimate thoughts of the writers. More importantly, however, we discover through their writing who God is. Which is just what they intended!

THE GOOD, THE BAD, AND THE FAMILY

Day 3 Exercise

READ PSALM 107:1-22.

> *Some wandered in desert wastes, finding no way. . . . Then they cried to the LORD in their trouble and he delivered them. . . . Let them thank the LORD.—Psalm 107:4, 6, 15*

REFLECT Another central Old Testament story is the forty-year exile of the Israelites to Babylon and their return to Jerusalem. Psalm 107 recounts a few of the thousands of stories drawn from Israelites who survived the return pilgrimage home.

Who in today's world comes to mind when you read these stories of survival and faith? Which story can you identify with in some way?

If you were to add a verse or a paragraph to this psalm drawn from your faith story, how would it read?

PRAY Thank the Lord for whatever sustained you in the worst of times.

ACT Write a prayer that will sustain you in hard times. Place it in your Bible at Psalm 107 so that you can turn to it the next time you are struggling.

> What do we and the people of the Bible have in common? The anxieties and joys of living; the sense of wonder and the resistance to it; the awareness of the hiding God and moments of longing to find a way to [God].[1]
>
> —Abraham Heschel

Day 3 Reading

A scene in the movie *Big Fish* shows young William Bloom in bed with chicken pox, talking to his father, Edward. Edward begins to tell William how he had to stay in bed for three years to combat his rapid growth spurt. The growth spurt made Edward the best baseball player, the unstoppable football player, the winning basketball player, the science fair genius, the boss of a lawn mowing company, a fire rescuer, and an overall hero who confronted the town's giant. Of course, William just wants to know the truth because these stories seem so unreal.

Our families have stories too—tales of bravery, love, shame, happiness, and difficulty. Some of our stories make us proud. Others leave us embarrassed, depressed, or wondering what really happened. The Bible's stories were passed from generation to generation as well. Just like anyone's family stories, there are good times, terrible times, and mysterious times.

Should Cain and Abel have gone to counseling before taking matters into their own hands? Could David's tale of impregnating his soldier's wife and assuring his death in battle be featured on an episode of talk-show television? And, let's be real, have *you* ever had a conversation with a burning bush?

The storytelling process of Bible times results in our having several versions of one story. We may wonder about the two Creation stories in chapters 1 and 2 of Genesis. The compiler of the Genesis material was not alive during Creation, so probably included two popular variations of the account. Instead of seeing the two stories as contradictory, we can view them as complementary. Both are spiritually true and speak of God creating everything for a good purpose.

The Gospel accounts give us four versions of the story of Jesus. We have four authors writing to four different audiences with four ways of telling the story. While the stories differ in some respects, they all proclaim the good news of the gospel, revealing the truth of God's gift to us in Jesus.

CHOOSE YOUR OWN ADVENTURE

Day 4 Exercise

READ LUKE 24:13-35.

While they were talking and discussing, Jesus himself came near and went with them, but their eyes were kept from recognizing him.
—Luke 24:16

REFLECT The central story of Christian faith concerns Jesus' life, death, and resurrection. The Emmaus road story tells of Christ in the lives of two disciples who undergo changes from (1) naive faith (before Jesus' crucifixion) to (2) loss of faith (verses 13-24) to (3) new and deeper faith (verses 25-35).

Which of these three phases in the story best describes where you find yourself right now? Record your insights.

PRAY Spend a few minutes in prayerful conversation with Christ about where you perceive his presence and where you do not perceive his presence in your life these days.

ACT Draw a picture of yourself in the Emmaus road story. Is Jesus walking with you? Do you recognize who he is?

> God is with us, exerting an influence on us whether we choose to pay attention or not.[2]
>
> —Martha Graybeal Rowlett

Day 4 Reading

When I was younger I really enjoyed the kind of books where you could choose your own adventure. In these fun, dramatic books you sometimes were given options for the next action in the plot.

At the bottom of a page I would read something like this: "The kidnappers are getting closer to the twins. If the twins keep running, turn to page 38; if the twins hide in a garbage dumpster, turn to page 107." These books were wonderful because I could select what seemed to be the happy ending or start all over if I was wrong.

Maybe God should have used this concept in biblical times. I imagine Samson might have liked to choose: "If Delilah will adore you, turn to page 10; if Delilah will betray you, turn to page 66." Maybe others would have liked to craft their stories differently. Jacob might not have cheated his brother out of his birthright. Even the two thieves on their crosses could have taken the option of convincing Jesus to use his powers and keep all three of them from dying.

But God was authoring a greater story than any of the characters could have chosen for themselves. This is the deeper story guiding our individual stories. Sometimes we want to choose our adventures too. Many of us would take the option of being accepted to our first college choice. Or it would be nice to have another option to our parents' divorce. If a friend at school dies, we want to write a different ending to the story.

Consider that through reading the Bible we are being both shaped by and crafted into the story of God. Consider that God is writing a larger, divine story in our lives right now. When do we trust God with the pen? When do we prefer to choose our own adventures? How do we see God's greater story working through each event in our lives?

CHRONOLOGY

Day 5 Exercise

READ GALATIANS 1:11–2:1.

You have heard, no doubt, of my earlier life in Judaism. . . . Then after three years I did . . . visit Cephas. . . . Then after fourteen years I went up to Jerusalem again with Barnabas.—Galatians 1:13, 18; 2:1

REFLECT The Christian story continues to unfold in the adventures of Paul and the other apostles. In Galatians, Paul tells of his own transformation in Christ that took place over many years as he searched for understanding and companionship in faith.

As you read Paul's story, notice the natural "chapters" in his journey. What do you feel Paul is searching for in each part of his story? With which parts of Paul's journey do you identify? What are you searching for?

PRAY Give thanks to God for Paul's faithfulness in each chapter of his life and pray that you will also find inspiration and strength for each chapter of your life.

ACT Check out a book or go to www.upperroom.org/methodx/thelife to learn about saints of the church and how they have lived faithfully.

Day 5 Reading

THE LOCATION: Paradise (aka Garden of Eden)

THE PLAYERS: Creator and Creation (oh, and that snake)

THE GAME: Life

THE STORY (in rap):

Tempted by the snake, Adam and Eve eat from the tree,
and, oh, the drama begins at this fall of humanity!
Their son Cain kills Abel, his very own brother.
Noah builds an ark to be safe from the water.
God tells old Abe and Sarah they'll have a son.
Abraham will build a new nation, and God will bless everyone.
But the Israelites land in Egypt and become slaves
until Moses frees them, putting Pharaoh's army into Red Sea graves.
The nation crosses the Jordan River but still disobeys.
They want a king, a fearless leader, to show them the way.
Saul, David, and Solomon each rule for awhile,
but God was the ruler the Israelites needed all the while.
When Solomon dies, the kingdom soon divides:
Ten tribes become Israel, and Judah gets two tribes.
Through good kings and bad kings, both kingdoms take a dive;
the northern kingdom cannot make it—nobody survives.
And the kingdom of Judah does not have it so easy.
The Babylonians come and place them in captivity.
Hundreds of years the Jews struggle to get things right,
and God promises a Savior, who will be the light.
So then Jesus comes wrapped in swaddling clothes—
the Son of God born to woman—with human eyes, ears, and toes.
Jesus heals and teaches, promises and preaches all over the land
with twelve disciples in tow and a following more than any man.
The Pharisees and Sadducees, upset by Jesus' clout,
plot and finally decide, "We have to take him out!"
He is crucified, dead, and buried but comes back on day three
(now this does not happen anywhere—except maybe on TV).
So the followers of Jesus become the church, waiting for him to come again.
And he will in final victory! Paradise will be restored in the end!

The End.
And the beginning.

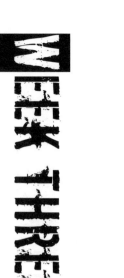

A WORD ABOUT THE WEEK

Daily reading and praying of scripture allows God to shape us and prepare us for pilgrimage. Reading and praying the Bible is our spiritual warm-up for the soul. Take time to quiet yourself before beginning each daily exercise. Ask God to shape you as you read. Use your journal to note new insights.

BEING STRETCHED AND CHALLENGED

Day 1   Exercise

READ GENESIS 3:1-13.

> *Now the serpent . . . said to the woman, "Did God say . . . ?"*
> *. . . But the* Lord *God called to the man, and said to him, "Where are you?"—Genesis 3:1, 9*

REFLECT This story speaks to the challenge of paying attention to God. First, read with your head. What does the story suggest about barriers to the kind of relationship God desires?

Second, read with your heart. Listen for the sound of God's voice in you. Pause at points along the way to allow at least one of these verses to search you personally.

- Verse 8: Where have you "heard the sound of the Lord God walking in the garden" of your life, and what do you hear?
- Verses 8-9: What are you hiding from? How would you answer God's call, "Where are you?"
- Verse 13: Speak God's question, "What is this that you have done?" Search for God's tone in asking. What does the question stir in you?

PRAY Listen for the sound of God's voice as you meditate. Pray aloud the responses of your heart to God.

ACT Choose one barrier in your relationship with God and commit to bring it down with the help of the Spirit.

Day 1 Reading

Remember a time when you did a lot of physical activity without stretching first? Maybe you were on vacation and did more walking than you expected. Maybe you decided to go for a jog but forgot to stretch. Maybe you were painting a room, and you didn't think about stretching at all. When this happens, sometimes your feet get weary, your legs get sore, and your arms ache. You think that you have done something wrong or that you're just not cut out for that particular activity, which may not be the case at all.

When we stretch, we warm our muscles in preparation for the ways we are going to use them. Some medical professionals suggest that we stretch every morning when we first awaken so that our bodies can warm up for movement. Athletes are always told to stretch before they begin their sport.

The pilgrimage is no different. As we journey toward the heart of God in our faith, we must stretch and exercise daily. We can know the Bible and hear about it every Sunday during the sermon. We can participate in small groups each week, where people study and share thoughts about the Bible. Yet, if we are not daily reading the Bible, praying the scripture, and allowing the Word of God to shape us, we are not going to be prepared for the pilgrimage.

Just like stretching before a long walk prepares the body to endure, praying scripture daily prepares the soul to endure. Reading and praying the Bible is our spiritual warm-up for the soul.

John Wesley, founder of the movement that became known as Methodism, understood this when he wrote,

> O begin! Fix some part of every day for private exercises. . . .
> Whether you like it or no, read and pray daily. It is for your life;
> there is no other way.[1]

EQUIPPED FOR THE PILGRIMAGE

Day 2 Exercise

READ GENESIS 32:22-32.

Jacob was left alone; and a man wrestled with him until daybreak.
—*Genesis 32:24*

REFLECT In this story, Jacob goes alone to the river where he wrestles with God and is changed. First, read with your head and with an eye for fact and context. For example, what does the name *Jacob* mean? What was Jacob worried about, and what did he need to wrestle with God about? (Look in Gen. 27 and 32:3-21.)

Second, read with your heart and with an ear for the voice of God in you. Meditate on one or more of these invitations:

- What part of you identifies with Jacob's need to get away from others to deal with some things?
- Where is a place you can really be alone with God? Imagine God waiting for you there.
- What do you and God need to wrestle about? What happens if you don't? What happens if God wins?

PRAY Put yourself in Jacob's place and imagine God asking you, "What is your name?" How would you name your life? How would God name the promise of your life?

ACT Look up the meaning of your name on www.behindthename.com. Or ask your parents why they chose your name. Hear God calling your name.

Day 2 Reading

A football player who gets on the field without a helmet and pads is out of his mind. At least he'll be out of his mind after getting slammed around enough times. A soccer player running on the field without cleats and a jersey will be asked to sit down no matter how good a player she is. To play the best game, everyone on the team needs to be equipped.

Some equipment is universal, and some reflects personal preference. For example, all guitar players have guitar strings, but some determine they also need a tuner, a psychedelic guitar strap, a capo, or a special pick.

As we continue our pilgrimage with reflective scripture practices, we should look at our necessary equipment as well. Some tools are essential. In other cases we can determine the need for ourselves. Consider the following tools for the journey.

BIBLE—Choosing a Bible for study and prayer is very important. Many translations are available. You want a version you can easily read and understand. Thumb through several at the bookstore. Often it's good to have more than one translation when you study.

CONCORDANCE—This reference book will tell you where in the Bible to find a specific word, subject, or person. A concordance allows you to do a word study quickly.

BIBLE COMMENTARIES—If you're studying a particular book of the Bible, you may want a commentary written by a biblical scholar to provide historical background and interpretation.

PENS AND HIGHLIGHTERS—Some people like to highlight key passages for easy reference. If you do not like writing in your Bible, try using small sticky notes to mark important passages.

JOURNAL—You will want to record your discoveries or write questions you may have. Depending on your needs, you may want to keep a biblical journal separate from your daily diary if you have one already.

OPEN HEART—It's vital to be equipped with a prayerful, open heart when studying scripture, so God can have a conversation with you through the Word.

BE PREPARED FOR THE PILGRIMAGE

Day 3 Exercise

READ PSALM 81.

O that my people would listen to me,
that Israel would walk in my ways!
—Psalm 81:13

REFLECT After the opening call to worship, this psalm expresses God's deep disappointment over our spiritual deafness and calls us again to listen for divine guidance.

First, read with your head. Notice ways the Lord is present but unnoticed in Israel's history (verses 5-16). What does the text say about the hearts of the Israelites?

Second, read with your heart and listen for the voice of God in you.

- Meditate on the "voice I had not known" (verse 5). Listen for the voice of that unseen Presence in your life, inviting a greater awareness.
- As you meditate on verses 5-16, wonder how God would tell the story of being quietly present in your life. Write a poem, draft a few lines, or draw an image that expresses your sense of God's quiet participation in your personal history.

PRAY "O that my people would listen to me. . . ." Practice a few minutes of being open in heart to whatever God might want to say.

ACT Find a couple of objects that symbolize your heart when it's open and listening versus when it's closed and stubborn (verse 12). Follow through on one little thing God would be pleased for you to do today.

Day 3 Reading

Time for the big race! I was a fairly new runner determined to run my first half-marathon, or 13.1 miles. I had never run more than ten miles at one time in my entire life, but I had trained and hoped I knew enough to finish the race.

I ate plenty of pasta the night before the race. Every runner's magazine suggested a good carbohydrate meal for fuel. On the morning of the race I took in a few pieces of fruit and some water. During the race people lined the road ready to give me orange wedges, carbohydrate bars, gel, water, or sports drinks. When the race finally ended (and it seemed like forever), a smorgasbord of healthy foods to refuel my body awaited the runners.

While a pilgrimage is not a race, it can be a long, sometimes difficult journey that expends spiritual and emotional energy. The soul needs to be refueled and fed by God's Word. When we study and pray with scripture, we feast on the Word of God as a way to revitalize our spirits.

We cannot afford to starve ourselves spiritually the way anorexia causes people to starve their bodies physically. We grow thin, frail, and weak when we do not eat, leading eventually to death. For our souls to grow robust and strong for this journey, we need to feast daily on the Bible. Otherwise we will starve our souls and kill our spirits. In fact, forget about your diet! Go for a second helping of the Word of God as often as you desire.

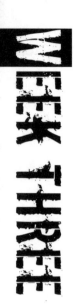

KNOWING THE PATH

Day 4 Exercise

READ JOHN 10:1-6.

I am the gate. Whoever enters by me will be saved, and will come in and go out and find pasture. The thief comes only to steal and kill and destroy. I came that they may have life, and have it abundantly.
—John 10:9-10

REFLECT This passage is about Jesus, the good shepherd who "calls his sheep by name and leads them out" to places of abundant life. First, read with your head, noticing all it says about differences between the good shepherd and the thief in the parable. List the differences.

Second, read with your heart. Listen for the voice of the good shepherd in your life.

- Where do you hear the trusted voice of the shepherd? What are its qualities?
- Where do you detect the voice of "the thief"? What are its qualities?
- Where or when is it hard for you to tell the difference?

PRAY Imagine the good shepherd saying to you, "*(Your name)*, I have come that *you* may have life and have it abundantly." What would that mean for you? Write what comes to mind.

ACT Think about a choice you have to make in the near future. Which choice will lead to the abundant life that the good shepherd desires for you?

Day 4 Reading

Since I drive to my house all the time and know how to get there, I don't always pay attention to the details of the route. So when someone asks how to find my house, it gets a little tricky:

"Take the exit after the billboard for some telephone company. I'm not sure which company, but the sign has a lady with really big hair on it. I think it should say 21st Avenue. But maybe not. Then go through a few lights. Turn right at the donut shop. Pass an elementary school and turn left, but immediately veer to the right when you see the fish statue on the corner . . ."

When I gave a friend these directions, he opted instead to use an online mapping service to find my house. It's not that he didn't value my experience and knowledge. He just knew he would need a map to find the path!

So it is on the pilgrimage. People who have gone before us—our parents, friends, pastors, and role models—can tell us about their journey. While we value their wisdom and experience, we also need the Bible as a path-finder with instructions on journeying closer to the heart of God.

Reading the Bible is not the only way to experience God. We encounter God every day in circumstances, other people, and nature. But biblical reflection allows us to see and understand God's truth, love, and direction better in daily life. The scriptures draw us closer to God and remind us of the path back to God's arms when we get lost. As the psalmist says, "Your word is a lamp to my feet and a light to my path" (Ps. 119:105).

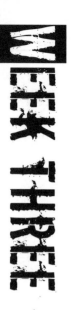

WEEK THREE SHAPED BY THE WORD ON PILGRIMAGE

THOSE WHO HAVE JOURNEYED AHEAD OF YOU

Day 5 Exercise

READ 2 TIMOTHY 1:1-7.

I am reminded of your sincere faith . . . that lived first in your grandmother Lois and your mother Eunice and now, I am sure, lives in you. For this reason I remind you to rekindle the gift of God that is within you.—2 Timothy 1:5-6

REFLECT As Timothy's spiritual mentor, Paul assures him, "I remember you constantly in my prayers night and day."

First, read with your head to understand the situation: How might you imagine Paul's relationship with Timothy, his mother, and his grandmother? What do you think Timothy's tears are all about (see verse 4)? What does "rekindle" mean?

Second, read with your heart, searching for the points where you identify with Paul or Timothy.

- Verse 3: Consider whether you, like Timothy, could benefit from having a spiritual mentor or faith friend like Paul. If you could chose any Bible character as a spiritual mentor, who would it be?
- Verse 4: "Recalling your tears," think about who would really listen to the cry of your heart. And who needs *you* to listen to their cry?
- Verses 5-6: Draw a picture of a fire, the fire of your faith. Is it burned out, a glowing ember, or a roaring flame? Picture what may be putting out the fire or what would rekindle it.

PRAY Give thanks for those whose hands have held you and blessed you with gifts of faith and love. Ask God for courage to reach out to those who need your encouragement and your blessing.

ACT Take a moment to make a phone call, write a note, or send an e-mail to one person who has blessed you or to someone who could use a blessing.

Day 5 Reading

In my dance class, my fellow dancers and I learn new choreography or techniques and then practice, practice, practice. Our instructor always tells us to watch videos and attend performances of some of the great dancers we admire. She says that by learning from the veterans, we will become better dancers.

So we watch videos of the professionals, noticing how they spin, paying attention to their stage presence, and noticing what mistakes they make and how they recover. We go to performances and observe how each dancer interprets the music. The pros train us to be better dancers even though we are just watching them.

A guitarist may listen to Jimi Hendrix and try to mimic his playing style. A missionary may read books about Mother Teresa. Aspiring business people might try to have an apprenticeship with Donald Trump. People who want to do well in a field pay close attention to the veterans who have gone before them.

Our biblical story offers many examples of people living faithfully. We see their struggles and their victories. Reading the book of Job gives us a glimpse of how someone who endured terrible suffering wrestled with God about his faith. Studying the beginning of Matthew lets us visit with Mary and watch her unfold to God's will. In reading the Gospels, we witness how Jesus loved people. We don't have to guess about what Jesus would do. We have examples of what he did.

Pondering scripture lets us be apprentices of the Christian life. We find models of the way to live. The Bible may not contain clear examples of every issue we face (I don't remember Jesus making a decision about where to go to college). But when we read the Bible, we learn how Jesus lived and how he made decisions. His example enlightens us on our own pilgrimage. When we study scripture, we learn from the veterans of the faith.

WEEK THREE SHAPED BY THE WORD ON PILGRIMAGE

Just as we walk with people, we can walk with the Word of God. When we meditate on scripture and write it on our heart, we learn to dwell in God's Word. The words are alive in our hearts to protect us, advise us, and encourage us along the path. Create some space in your days this week to walk with the Word through these daily exercises. Be sure to note your thoughts in your journal.

DAY AND NIGHT

Day 1 Exercise

READ PSALM 23.

> *The Lord is my shepherd, I shall not want.*
> *He makes me lie down in green pastures;*
> *he leads me beside still waters; he restores my soul.*
> —Psalm 23:1-3

REFLECT Psalm 23 is a good place to begin with meditation because you may know some verses by memory. Today you will practice spiritual focus with a verse of scripture as a way to prepare for listening to God.

Read Psalm 23 again aloud. On this second reading, take time to dwell on the words and images in each verse. Select one verse that is rich in meaning for you. Meditate slowly on that verse, repeating it, savoring the words. Close your eyes and visualize it; draw or color what you see. Explore what this verse says to you.

PRAY Pray with open hands before God, sharing what the verse touches in you. Ask what gift the Spirit wants you to receive, and wait in silence while reciting the verse.

ACT Pray your sacred verse today as a breath prayer. For example, "The Lord is my shepherd" (*while breathing in*), "I shall not want" (*while breathing out*); or, "he leads me beside still waters" (*breathing in*), "he restores my soul" (*breathing out*). Repeat your verse throughout the day.

Day 1 Reading

Have you ever had a song stuck in your head? Maybe you hear a catchy tune on the radio early in the morning. It doesn't matter if it is your favorite song or one you don't like at all. By lunchtime, you want your friends to sing a song—anything but the one from the radio that morning—so you can get it out of your head.

Other things get stuck in our head too. When we have a crush on someone, we may have him or her on our mind all the time. We know his schedule, when she has exams, what time his football practice starts, how many brothers she has. When reading a really good book, we may have certain characters in our mind. We wonder how their story will end, and we think about how we can't wait to pick up the book again.

The things on our mind stay with us. We allow them to be a part of who we are and to rest in our thoughts all day and sometimes even through the night. The book of Psalms opens with these words: "Happy are those who . . . delight . . . in the law of the LORD, and on his law they meditate day and night" (1:1-2). When we allow the Word of God to get stuck in our heart and mind, we think of it all day. The scriptures become a part of who we are, how we speak, what we do. The Word walks with us daily and gives us comfort, direction, advice, reminders, and help throughout the day. Fixing our gaze upon the Lord draws us nearer to God.

To sense the presence of God in the Bible, one must learn to be present to God in the Bible.[1]

—Abraham Heschel

WEEK FOUR

WALKING WITH THE WORD

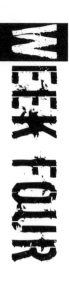

MEDITATION AS DISCOVERY

Day 2 Exercise

READ PSALM 27:1-5.

> The LORD is my light and my salvation;
>   whom shall I fear?
> The LORD is the stronghold of my life;
>   of whom shall I be afraid?
> —Psalm 27:1

REFLECT Arrange your space for meditation with a candle. Light the candle as a reminder of God's presence. Then return to Psalm 27 and read verse 1 only, one phrase at a time. Make verse 1 the focus of meditation for ten minutes in the following way.

Reflect on the meaning of each phrase or word, or dwell on each image. As you gaze at the burning candle, explore the qualities of the flame and what that flame tells you about "the Lord," "my light," "and my salvation." In this way, prepare space for God within you.

PRAY Respond to the question "Of whom shall I be afraid?" Tell the Lord about your fears; name what controls you or what you fear you cannot live without. Then listen to the Lord with an open and freshly emptied heart; let the Lord's "light" and "salvation" fill you.

Rest in the "stronghold" of God's presence. Give thanks for whatever gift you have received. Record your experience.

ACT Place a candle in your room as a reminder of God's presence, light, and salvation.

Day 2 Reading

I was so excited about my first yoga class! I brought my yoga mat, a blanket, and my own eye pillow. I wore yoga pants, brought a yoga jacket I had purchased, and was wearing a yoga tank top. Yes, I got a little carried away. But I was really looking forward to this experience.

The class did not disappoint me. I enjoyed the workout. I felt relaxed. Then the teacher said it was time to cool down with meditative practices. Oh no! Here I was all decked out and prepared for yoga, but I forgot about the "Om"!

Thoughts flooded my mind: *I don't meditate! How do I escape before the "Om"? If they hurry and shut their eyes, maybe I can crawl out the door.* Of course, I did not make a smooth exit out of the room. I sat there saying nothing as others chanted. Mostly I stared at everyone, terribly uncomfortable with this Eastern form of meditation.

When I explored the idea of meditation further, though, I realized that I already meditated more than I knew. As Christians, we build on the ancient Jewish practice of meditation, reflecting on and repeating God's Word. Psalm 143:5 declares, "I meditate on all your words and consider what your hands have done" (NIV). Meditation is a way to discover more of God, a way to let the Holy Spirit guide us into deeper insight. We invite God's Word to be on our mind, to walk with us throughout the day. By pondering these ideas, we draw closer to their essence. Tomorrow's reading will provide a helpful guide to meditation on scripture.

We certainly encounter the Holy outside of scripture, but true relationship with God develops from contemplating what we learn about God through the Bible. When we meditate on scripture, we contemplate the truth of God's Word. This contemplation gives us a chance to focus on God's will and way so that they become a part of who we are. Meditation draws us nearer to the heart of God. In discovering more about God on this pilgrimage, we also discover we are children of God made in the divine image.

DON'T WORRY, BE MEDITATIVE!

Day 3 Exercise

READ NUMBERS 6:22-27.

> *The LORD bless you and keep you;*
> *the LORD make his face to shine upon you, and be gracious to you;*
> *the LORD lift up his countenance upon you, and give you peace.*
> *—Numbers 6:24-26*

REFLECT The Lord gives this blessing to Moses to give in turn to Aaron and his sons. It is meant to bless the Israelites on pilgrimage to the Promised Land.

Write the blessing (verses 24-26) on a card. If any word puzzles you, look up its meaning. Arrange your meditation space by placing the card where you can see it beside the candle.

Meditate on the blessing for ten minutes, preparing your inner space for God who is with you. Recite the blessing phrase by phrase; imagine God doing what the words describe for you and for others. Savor each image.

PRAY Talk with the Lord as the words move you. Offer to God whatever surfaces in your mind or heart as you recite the blessing. Soak in the blessing's promises.

ACT Cherish the gift of God's presence in this moment. As you walk through your house, school, or neighborhood today, carry the blessing and find ways to bless all you see.

> **If you turn your back on all outward consolation you will be able to**
> **contemplate heavenly things and often exult in them.[2]**
>
> **—Thomas à Kempis**

NOTE: *To prepare for tomorrow's exercise, look for a picture or icon of Jesus.*

Day 3 Reading

So, meditation is no problem. We simply think about something, right? Well, not necessarily. People think about things all day in different ways. For example, Delores moved to Los Angeles with her family from a much smaller town in the southern part of the United States. While she's excited about new opportunities for the family there, she thinks a lot about the violence and crime in parts of Los Angeles. She thinks of the possible muggings and about people breaking into her house.

Delores allows these thoughts to sit with her all day long. But she is not meditating; she is worrying and holding onto fear. Delores has moments of peace, but her thoughts more often reflect her anxieties.

When we meditate, we are not worrying about spiritual matters or how God may respond to a situation. Nor do we worry about whether we will be able to live up to God's will, or even whether we will understand scripture.

Meditation on scripture, in fact, provides a refuge from stress and worry. Through meditation we spend time resting and trusting in God.

Sample Meditation Guide

Pray Begin your conversation with God, asking for help to rest in the Word.

Read Choose a short passage of scripture. Read it slowly.

Reflect Contemplate the scripture. What does it say to you? What images do you find? What does it tell you about God? Let the ideas linger in your heart and mind; don't be in a hurry to come to a conclusion.

Rest Consider what image or insight you can take from the scripture and simply rest in it. Rest in what you understand or don't understand. Rest in what you learned about God. Keep it with you all day.

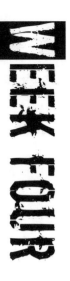

TAKING SCRIPTURE TO HEART

Day 4 Exercise

READ MATTHEW 16:13-16 AND ANY STUDY NOTES ON THE PASSAGE YOUR BIBLE PROVIDES.

> *Now when Jesus came into the district of Caesarea Philippi, he asked his disciples, "Who do people say that the Son of Man is?" And they said, "Some say John the Baptist, but others Elijah, and still others Jeremiah or one of the prophets." He said to them, "But who do you say that I am?" Simon Peter answered, "You are the Messiah, the Son of the living God."*
> —Matthew 16:13-16

REFLECT If possible, place a picture or icon of Jesus where you can look at it in your meditation space. Slowly read each phrase in the scripture passage above, imagining the scene, wondering what God wants to say or ask you today.

Reflect on Jesus' two questions. Imagine Jesus asking you personally, "Who do people today say I am?" Ponder this; write your thoughts. Then imagine Jesus asking, "Who do *you* say I am?" Explore what you affirm and question, believe and wonder about. Listen to what rises from your heart.

PRAY Respond to Jesus personally now. Gazing at the picture or icon, speak with Jesus from your mind and heart. Be honest, trusting he already knows you through and through but wants a living, growing relationship. Listen for inner promptings of the Spirit.

ACT Rest in God and receive Jesus' remarkable trust in you to be part of his church. Resolve to live by your faith. Record your insights or leading.

Day 4 Reading

Remember that the book of Psalms opens, "Happy are those who . . . delight . . . in the law of the LORD, and on his law they meditate day and night" (Ps. 1:1-2). Another psalm entreats, "Let the words of my mouth and the meditation of my heart be acceptable to you, O LORD, my rock and my redeemer" (Ps. 19:14). Jesus of Nazareth doubtless spent many hours meditating on the Hebrew scriptures, just as other rabbis did. His use of scripture in engaging his critics makes this clear.

Based on these early Hebrew practices of meditation, the Christian practice of scriptural meditation blossomed in the deserts of Egypt and Arabia among hermits and monks of the fourth through sixth centuries.

These desert fathers and mothers, as they are called, sought purity of heart in order to see God more clearly. Few of these devout individuals in the early centuries of the church would have owned complete Bibles or been able to read them. Yet the sayings of the desert fathers and mothers (the written record of their advice and commentary) often describe the benefits of meditating on scripture. Many of these hardy souls had learned scripture by heart. They memorized large portions of the Psalms and the Gospels in particular, from hearing them read in weekly worship gatherings or learning them from monks and hermits who could read.

Both individually and together, the monks spoke scripture aloud, mulled over the words in their minds, "chewed" on them, and slowly "digested" them. This practice helped them gradually abandon themselves to God, as the Spirit strengthened and transformed their lives.[3]

In oral cultures, people rely on memory. But even in our culture we can commit scripture to memory. When we take it into our hearts for safekeeping, scripture can nourish and guide us and eventually transform our lives as well.

WEEK FOUR

WALKING WITH THE WORD

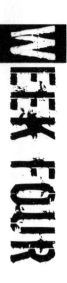

WALKING WITH THE WORD

Day 5 Exercise

READ ROMANS 8:31-39.

No, in all these things we are more than conquerors through him who loved us. For I am convinced that neither death, nor life, nor angels, nor rulers, nor things present, nor things to come, nor powers, nor height, nor depth, nor anything else in all creation, will be able to separate us from the love of God in Christ Jesus our Lord.—Romans 8:37-39

REFLECT Reflect on a verse you choose from today's reading. Write it out. Draw a picture of what it means to be separated from God's love. Think about all the ways that separation is real for you or others in the world. Draw a second picture of what it means to trust that "nothing can separate us from the love of Christ." Light a candle in your prayer space. Set the pictures by the candle to see as you meditate on your chosen verse for a few minutes.

PRAY Respond to this passage with prayer as you are led. Honestly speak with God about circumstances in which you or others you know do feel separated from God's love. Listen for what God says about these situations.

ACT Rest in God's presence as you offer yourself and your concerns to God. Receive courage to bring others the assurance "that neither death, nor life . . . nor anything else in all creation, will be able to separate us from the love of God in Christ Jesus our Lord" (verses 38-39).

Day 5 Reading

In the popular novel and film trilogy *The Lord of the Rings,* the hero, Frodo, takes a journey from his home in the Shire to the dreaded land of Mordor to get rid of a powerful and destructive magic ring. His journey is a pilgrimage, because he has a specific destination and higher purpose for his journey. Three traveling companions stay with Frodo for most of the journey: Merry, Pippin, and Sam. They protect, advise, and assist him on his long quest.

As people wandering on earth with the destiny of returning to God, we are pilgrims as well. We encounter many other pilgrims who take the journey with us, protecting, advising, and helping us along the path. Some of these companions may walk long stretches of the pilgrimage with us.

Have you ever thought of the Bible as one of those companions? It may not have legs, arms, or ears, but it is a companion all the same. Just as we walk with other people, we can walk with the Word of God. When we meditate on scriptures and write them on our heart, we learn to dwell in God's Word. We can dialogue with the words just like having a conversation with our parents or friends. The words are alive in our heart to protect us, advise us, and help us along the path.

Long after we close our Bibles, we can still meditate on God's Word and glory. We are invited to seek God in our everyday living. With God's words in our heart and our eyes open to the Spirit, we can meditate throughout the day.

When scripture shapes our imagination, we begin to think of our future in a new way. We learn to look at every situation in our lives through the lens of the gospel message. This week's daily exercises encourage you to work mental and spiritual "muscles" that you rarely use. Be open to what the Holy Spirit has to say to you through experiencing scripture in this way. Use your journal to note new thoughts and insights.

IMAGINE!

Day 1 Exercise

READ GENESIS 1:1–2:9.

These are the generations of the heavens and the earth when they were created.—Genesis 2:4

REFLECT The ancient authors of these two Creation stories have different mental pictures of Creation. Can you see them? In the first story, the human being stands at the pinnacle of a creative development pyramid. In the second, the human being is the center of a circle of life. The first moves from chaos to Creation; the second moves from barren desert to lush garden for human habitation. As you reread the passages, try to visualize what each author sees. Sketch these different visions on two adjacent pages.

PRAY Which picture of Creation stirs your imagination or seems most relevant to you? Considering both stories, imagine a conversation with God about our world and how we are caring for the environment. What would the God we see in Genesis 1 feel, say, or do? What would the God of Genesis 2 feel, say, or do? Ask God to be present in the hurting places of the world.

ACT Look at the world today through the eyes of God the Creator. How will you treat your world differently today?

Day 1   Reading

Imagine there is no life, no breath—only clay and the Sculptor.

Imagine hands digging through earth to find the finest of clay for the future masterpiece.

Imagine these tender hands molding the clay, delicately and intricately. These hands correct any mistakes and perfect any flaws for the masterpiece.

Imagine the Sculptor smiling at the finished piece, delighted by the beautiful image.

Imagine the Sculptor kissing the precious creation and breathing life into it.

Imagine!

God has an amazing imagination! With no designs to mimic and no models to copy, God imagines and speaks into being the trees, birds, living persons. God creates the sounds of ocean waves, wind through leaves, and voices singing praise. God writes the stories of our life. God is, indeed, a sculptor, composer, and author. As the Creator of all things, our Maker is the originator of creativity!

Being made in the image of God, the Creator, we are designed to create too. We can nurture our imagination and use it to open our faith wider.

At times we need to study scripture to better understand God's message. But at other times, as we have been exploring, we need to meditate on the Word to draw closer to God and seek guidance. One form of active meditation involves the creative use of our imagination. We think of what it might be like to stand inside some of the biblical stories. Or we read a psalm and sing it as we imagine the psalmist may have sung it. Maybe we read the Creation story and try to imagine what it was like for God to create the world. The possibilities are endless when we approach the scriptures creatively. There is no end to our vivid imaginations!

God gives you dreams, creativity, and imagination as beautiful gifts. Let the Spirit use them to broaden your spiritual senses.

SENSORY READING

Day 2 Exercise

READ GENESIS 6:9-22; 7:11-16, EMPLOYING ALL YOUR SENSES.

Now the earth was corrupt in God's sight, and the earth was filled with violence. . . . And God said to Noah, "I have determined to make an end of all flesh, for the earth is filled with violence because of them; now I am going to destroy them along with the earth. Make yourself an ark of cypress wood; make rooms in the ark, and cover it inside and out with pitch."—Genesis 6:11-14

REFLECT The story of Noah and the ark relates God's deep disappointment with the way life on earth was turning out. God decides to destroy everything and start over with a few good representative samples of life. Read imaginatively with your senses. What do you see? What do you smell? What do you hear and feel?

What do you sense God is feeling when God says to Noah (verse 13), "I have determined to make an end of all flesh, for the earth is filled with violence because of them"? What picture of violence do you envision God seeing?

Imagine being a privileged soul with Noah and his family in the ark. What do you all talk about for 150 days? What are you sad or sorry about? What are you glad about? How are you going to help make sure life on earth works this time around?

PRAY Ask God to inspire individuals, organizations, world leaders, and the church to treat one another with mercy, kindness, and justice so that God might never feel the same despair over humanity.

ACT Read the newspaper or watch the news today and pray for a life restored to wholeness in each situation.

Day 2 Reading

Have you ever wondered what the meal tasted like when Jesus fed the multitude in Matthew 14:13-21? Were the fish steamed, fried, or sautéed and garnished with lemon wedges? Were they dried and salted or served raw? What did they smell like? What did people do when Jesus multiplied the loaves and fish? Did they "ooh" and "aah" at the sight of the miracle? Or were they amazed into silence? Did they sit patiently waiting for the disciples to distribute the meal? Or did some break in line for food because their stomachs were growling ferociously?

Whenever we wonder about such questions, we're diving into the scriptures with our imagination. It is a blessing to approach the text in this way because it places us inside the biblical stories. Sometimes you may be a fly on the wall, observing and listening to conversations. Other times you may be an actual character in the midst of the action. Either way, this method of approaching the Bible allows you to connect your memory and experience with the meaning of the story through imagination.

This approach, sometimes called the Ignatian method of reading, engages all five of our senses. We see, hear, smell, taste, and touch everything in the passage. When reading about the Exodus from Egypt, we may see looks of shock on people's faces as the sea parts. We might hear cheers explode through the crowd as they realize, *We don't have to swim to the other side!* We might smell the salt water or imagine the taste of sand for those so excited they begin kissing the ground! We might feel the seabed between our toes or a tiny child's hand clutching ours.

As we read with such imagination, we identify with the experience of those who lived these events and find greater meaning in them for our own lives. We not only get to hear what Jesus did but even delve into the mind of Christ and imagine what he was thinking, feeling, and hoping in his ministry. As we imagine his inner life, it begins to shape our own.

GUIDED MEDITATION

Day 3 Exercise

READ LUKE 1:26-38.

The angel said to her, "Do not be afraid, Mary, for you have found favor with God. And now, you will conceive in your womb and bear a son, and you will name him Jesus."—Luke 1:26-31

REFLECT This is a story about the way God sought to start life over and recreate the world through the birth of Jesus Christ to an adolescent girl. Read the story again, putting yourself in Mary's place. Try to imagine yourself as Mary, hearing the angel's message.

What do you actually experience? How do you respond to the angel's greeting and explanation of what is going on? How is the life of Jesus conceived in you? Jot down your thoughts.

PRAY Imagine that God has chosen you to be a vehicle of new life in the world today. What does it mean for you to say, "Let it be with me according to your word" as Mary did? Talk with God about what you need to do to be a vehicle of Christ's life to the world.

ACT Write "Let it be with me according to your word" on a card or piece of paper and place it in your wallet, or create a screensaver with these words for your phone or computer. Consider your actions today in light of this prayer.

Day 3 Reading

At the end of our campus ministry meeting, we were invited to find a cozy place in the room to relax and meditate. I found my comfortable space on the carpet, closed my eyes, and listened to our leader.

Heather read the story of the crucifixion from John's Gospel. I'd always heard this text proclaimed in a loud voice, but Heather spoke softly. I had to really quiet myself to hear her. After reading, Heather asked us to breathe in and out deeply. She told us to tense every muscle and hold them tight, then release our muscles so they were absolutely relaxed.

"Now imagine you're with the crowds watching Jesus on the way to Golgotha," Heather said. "You see him carrying his own cross, stumbling on the road. You see how he's already been beaten and bruised. What are you feeling? What do you wish you could do?"

It was difficult to imagine this and not feel guilty for standing still. Surely I could be the one who says, "Stop!" instead of "Crucify him!"

"Then follow the crowd and watch as the soldiers crucify Jesus. You see the men carrying large nails. You see the blood trickle from Jesus' wrists as he is nailed to the wood. What are you feeling? What do you want to do? Cry? Run away?"

I shiver. I'm not cold but horrified. Still I wonder if I will move and throw my body over this innocent man or if I will just allow this brutal murder.

"After the soldiers divide the Lord's clothing, the crowds begin to leave. You notice three women and a man near the cross. It's Jesus' mother, her sister, Mary of Magdala, and a disciple. What do you observe on their faces? What are you feeling? What do you want to do?"

They love this man, and I know why they love him. He is our Lord. I want to stand with them, mourn with them, and comfort them.

"You continue watching as Jesus says he is thirsty. Soldiers hold a soaked sponge to his dry mouth. Then you hear Jesus' last word and watch him take his last breath. What are you feeling? What do you want to do?"

I feel great pain for Jesus' suffering. Then I am reminded of the story beyond the Cross—that he arose from the dead. I am reminded that he did this for our freedom. I let go of the guilt and am overwhelmed with gratitude.

WEEK FIVE ALLOWING THE WORD TO SHAPE IMAGINATION

CREATIVE EXPRESSION THROUGH SCRIPTURE READING

Day 4 Exercise

READ LUKE 13:10-17.

When Jesus saw her, he called her over and said, "Woman, you are set free from your ailment." When he laid his hands on her, immediately she stood up straight and began praising God.—Luke 13:10-13

REFLECT This woman became a new person when Jesus healed her on the Sabbath over the objection of the synagogue leader. Imagine this woman's life before she met Jesus. What could have bent her over? How did others treat her?

After the woman was healed, what song might she have sung? What poem might she have written? What picture might she have created to celebrate her healing? Write or draw your imaginings in your journal.

PRAY Hold your journal or picture and lift it to God. Imagine this same healing and celebration for someone in your life who is hurting.

ACT Think of someone who could benefit from the acceptance and healing available through Jesus. Invite him or her to church with you this week.

Day 4 Reading

One morning I read:

> *And all of us, with unveiled faces, seeing the glory of the Lord as*
> *though reflected in a mirror, are being transformed into the same image*
> *from one degree of glory to another; for this comes from the Lord, the*
> *Spirit.—2 Corinthians 3:18*

The word *unveiled* captured me. If my face were truly unveiled, I could see
the glory of the Lord reflected in me. But I wrestled with being unveiled. If I
were absolutely naked before God, wouldn't God see all my flaws alongside
my goodness? Everything would be confessed to God if I were unveiled.

I contemplated this. Nakedness is rarely acceptable. It's illegal to be
naked in public. We have nightmares about being naked while making
speeches in front of a crowd. People often wear invisible masks at school,
work, and even church, pretending things are fine when they are not. So
this idea of being unveiled in order to see God's glory proved hard for me.
Then I opened my journal to write. I'll let you peek into it:

> Naked, Lord.
> If I were to drop my clothing before you,
> would I then know your glory?
> Or would I rush to cover pieces of me
> with tiny hands?
> Or wrap my left knee
> over its right partner
> as if this might keep my secrets
> Veiled?

On the page with this poem I colored and painted and used magazine
clippings to further illustrate these thoughts and illuminate the scripture.

I am not a great artist (unless stick figures count). I can play a few
chords on the guitar and can make a ball out of Play-Doh. So I could avoid
real creativity in my offerings to God. But faith and creative expression
accompany each other. King David wrote songs and poems. Spiritual
icons are painted by monks in direct response to prayer and scripture.
Worshipers dance and play music to praise God (Ps. 150). We can interact
with the Bible through our own modes of creative expression.

ALLOWING SCRIPTURE TO SHAPE OUR IMAGINATIONS

Day 5 Exercise

READ LUKE 14:12-24.

But when you give a banquet, invite the poor, the crippled, the lame, and the blind. And you will be blessed, because they cannot repay you, for you will be repaid at the resurrection of the righteous.—Luke 14:13-14

REFLECT The kingdom of God is like someone inviting people on the margins to a great dinner party. Reflect on this parable and the point Jesus is making to religious people.

Imagine Jesus coming to your church and asking if he can use the facility to throw a "Thy Kingdom Come on Earth" dinner party. Who would be invited? Who would come?

Imagine Jesus in your place or as the leader of your youth group, campus ministry, or small group. How might he put the parable into action in your community?

PRAY Pray that God would reveal to you ways to include people of all kinds in your care. Listen to God in silence. What possibilities do you begin to see? Note them in your journal.

ACT Take your ideas to your pastor or your small group to discuss the possibilities.

Day 5 Reading

A youth group studied the parable of the banquet found in Luke 14:12-24. They explored what it meant to be kind to those who are less fortunate and how to be hospitable without expecting anything in return. The teenagers seemed interested in the lesson.

At the end of the meeting, their leader announced that the following week would be the annual summer kick-off party. There would be a cookout with lots of food, fun games, and prizes. "Invite someone if you'd like," she said.

The next Sunday many of the youth brought friends from school who don't normally come to the meetings. Kenya was a little late for the party, but she made it with her guests. When volunteering at the church's food pantry that year, Kenya had noticed a woman and her two children coming to get food every few weeks. Kenya played with the children as the mother collected food. She learned that the family was homeless and visiting shelters until they could get back on their feet.

After studying the parable, Kenya was excited to see this family at church again. She knew exactly who she wanted to be her guests at the youth party and was thrilled when the woman accepted her invitation.

When reading scripture, we learn to imagine ourselves back in the biblical settings, but we can also imagine translating those settings to our current lives. Kenya imagined that their youth party was the grand banquet Jesus described. She imagined what it would mean to be like Christ in this situation. She could invite any of her good friends who would have fun at the meeting. Or she could invite this family who might never pay her back but who needed food and fellowship more than anything right now.

When scripture shapes our imagination, we can create more than artwork or music. We begin to create a new future by imagining ways to look at every situation in our lives through the lens of the gospel message.

We can experience scripture in more ways than reading it silently to ourselves. This week we will explore several approaches or methods that bring the Bible alive in groups and community settings. Be open to experiencing the Word in new ways. Have your journal handy for jotting down notes and ideas.

READ ALOUD

Day 1 Exercise

READ PSALM 130.

> I wait for the LORD, my soul waits,
>   and in his word I hope;
> my soul waits for the LORD
>   more than those who watch for the morning,
>   more than those who watch for the morning.
> —Psalm 130:5-6

REFLECT Read the psalm aloud three times. On the first reading, try to express the psalm as though these were your own words. Search for a way to say them from your heart. Take note of which verses or sections of the psalm you connect with most.

For the second reading, speak aloud only the verses selected above (verses 5-6). Again, read with feeling. Make the words your own. How do they touch your life? What do they express for you? Write it down.

For the third reading, say aloud the part you are finding most meaningful. Listen for points where you sense an invitation or hear a call.

PRAY Rewrite a verse of the psalm in your own words to express your personal prayer.

ACT As you make decisions today, pay attention to your heart's desire.

Day 1 Reading

It's the concert of the year by your favorite band. The instruments and microphones have been checked. The only thing left is for the group to get onstage and perform. The band members run onstage as the crowd's rumble of conversation turns to screams. There's clapping, yelling, and even some fainting; you're wishing the band would open with your favorite song. Right when you think you cannot stand it any longer, they hand out sheet music with chords for every one of their songs. The remainder of the show is silent while the entire audience holds the sheet music. The concert of the year! You have music on a page, but the *sound* is missing!

So many parts of scripture are lyrical: songs, poems, prayers, and chants. They should be shouted or whispered or carried with a tune. The texts are written on a page, and there is a time for approaching them silently. Reading the scriptures aloud, however, can add a fullness and richness to the words. It develops the context and evokes intended emotions. Try reading the Bible aloud and with energy.

We often read the Bible aloud in group settings. Sometimes we divide the passage into sections, and each person takes a part. At other times we read an entire passage alone in front of a Sunday school class or the whole congregation. When we know in advance that we will be reading a text, we should practice. If we can become familiar with the passage, we'll be prepared if we have to read something like "Shealtiel begot Zerubbabel." Getting familiar with the reading reduces the anxiety sometimes associated with reading aloud.

But of course we don't always have time to prepare to read. When the college chaplain asks you at the last minute to read at a campus ministry meeting, you may only have time to find the passage. Even then, you can read loudly, boldly, and with the confidence of a believer. Remember that scripture, like music, should be heard.

GROUP *LECTIO*

Day 2 Exercise

READ ISAIAH 40:1-5.

Comfort, O comfort my people, says your God.
—Isaiah 40:1

REFLECT Using the text above, practice an approach to *lectio divina* (meditative reading of scripture) that works just as well for an individual as for a group. It involves reading the passage three times.

- With the first reading, listen for a word, verse, or image that God seems to be giving you to consider more deeply or that simply stands out for you. Write it down. Memorize it. For example, "Comfort, O comfort my people."

- With the second reading, listen for the verse, phrase, or image that touches your life in some way. Explore the connection you see or feel. For example, "'Speak tenderly to Jerusalem' brings to mind a couple of friends who messed up big-time, along with my hope that God, parents, and school will have mercy and give them another chance."

- With the third reading, listen for an invitation or call—to do something, make a change, or pay more attention to a part of your life. For example, "I hear an invitation to 'prepare the way of the Lord' for my two friends in the midst of their 'wilderness,' to be a friend and 'speak tenderly' to them even if nobody else will."

PRAY Pray to God about the invitation or call that you hear.

ACT As a way to accept God's invitation, think of one action you can take this week to live out your call. Resolve to act on it.

Day 2 Reading

Mark Yaconelli has breathed new life into ministry with young people, pointing to our craving for authentic spirituality as opposed to entertainment. Through the Youth Ministry and Spirituality Project (1997–2004) Mark developed and introduced groups to the "liturgy for discernment," a process that emphasizes a safe space for people to listen to one another and for God.

Often in this way of listening, the group uses the spiritual practice of *lectio divina* or sacred reading. In his book *Contemplative Youth Ministry*, Yaconelli tells a brief story about the impact of group *lectio* for a Lutheran youth group in St. Paul, Minnesota. The youth pondered together the biblical accounts of Moses and his leading the Hebrew people to a new land.

> Before we began to practice the liturgy for discernment, we had a youth room with a pool table right in the middle of it. The room looked like a recreation room. As we began to pray and share together and discuss the question, "What is God's call for us?" we began to sense that we needed to create a youth space that was more sacred and less focused on entertainment or recreation. We shared this with the kids and asked them to pray about it. We were totally surprised when they said they sensed the same thing. So together we dismantled the pool table and had a month of meetings in which we talked about sacred space. We did Bible studies on Moses and the Holy Land and other kinds of lessons that referred to sacred space. Eventually, one of the kids designed a big butterfly that we all painted on one of the walls. We repainted the room as part of a prayer service. When we finished, we all just sat in the room—adults and youth—in awe at what God had led us to do. Now when kids bring their friends to the youth room, they point out the verses and images on the walls. They tell them how the room used to be just a recreation room. They tell the other kids like they're telling them something sacred has happened. And something sacred has happened.[1]

WEEK SIX

MEDITATING ON THE WORD TOGETHER

GROUP IGNATIAN READING

Day 3 Exercise

READ MARK 3:1-6.

Then he said to them, "Is it lawful to do good or to do harm on the sabbath, to save life or to kill?" But they were silent. He looked around at them with anger; he was grieved at their hardness of heart and said to the man, "Stretch out your hand." He stretched it out, and his hand was restored.—Mark 3:4-5

REFLECT Build on yesterday's approach. Today pay special attention to using your senses as you read.

- With the first reading, just get an idea of what's happening in the story and who all the characters are.
- With the second reading, activate your senses. Pause after each verse to picture the action and hear the voices. For example, imagine what "a man who had a withered hand" looked like. Visualize the Pharisees trying to trap Jesus. See and hear Jesus calling the man forward. Let yourself sense the feelings of each character as well.
- With the third reading, imagine you are the man with the withered hand. Hear Jesus calling you to "come forward" and to "stretch out your hand." What does the withered hand represent in your life— perhaps some part of you that feels embarrassing or useless or that you want to hide?

PRAY In prayer, visualize offering your hand to Jesus: "stretch it out" for Jesus to touch with healing love.

ACT How would you act differently today if the part of you that causes pain or shame were restored? Try acting this way!

Day 3 Reading

The Ignatian method of reading the Bible, developed by Ignatius of Loyola (sixteenth century), is sensory reading. By engaging the five senses, this method takes us inside scripture with active imagination. Ignatian reading can be fun in a group setting. Think of it as creating a play.

When using the Ignatian method in a group, begin by assigning senses to different group members. For example, a group is reading Mark 14:3-6. One member reads the passage simply thinking of the scents in the passage. She may consider the smell of the food at the table in Simon's home. She may imagine the overwhelming fragrance of the nard. Another member will think about touch. He may focus on the smooth coolness of the alabaster jar or the touch of anointing that Jesus felt from the woman. Another will concentrate on the sounds in this passage: the sound of the breaking jar, the silence after the jar was broken, the scolding that followed. Then the group will discuss the story, and the members will report on the senses they focused on in the passage.

Then it's time for casting. The narrator reads all the descriptive parts, and the characters read dialogue and act out the scene. The cast for Mark 14:3-6 might look like this: narrator, Jesus, woman, disciples, servants. If the group is large, there can be plenty of people around the table. Because the group will have established the setting according to the senses already, the actors have their directions for the play. Now the group is fully participating in the biblical story!

PERSONALIZING SCRIPTURE

Day 4 Exercise

SELECT AND READ ONE OF THESE PASSAGES: MATTHEW 11:28-30; JOHN 3:16; OR ROMANS 8:31-39.

REFLECT Now personalize the passage of scripture you have chosen. Either speak it or write it (or a portion) as though it were addressed to you personally. Feel free to adapt the text to your situation.

For example, one youth personalized Romans 8:38-39 to say: "I am convinced that neither my grades, nor boys, nor parents, nor even my coach . . . will be able to steal away God's love and acceptance of me as I am."

PRAY Read what you have written again as a statement of faith, and lift it to God as your prayer.

ACT Take this statement of faith with you today, pulling it out in moments of sadness or doubt.

> It is never sufficient simply to have read God's Word. It must penetrate deep within us, dwell in us, like the Holy of Holies in the Sanctuary.[2]
> —Dietrich Bonhoeffer

Day 4 Reading

Once with a Bible study group I read 1 Corinthians 13:4-7: "Love is patient; love is kind; love is not envious or boastful. . . ." After reading the entire passage, we talked about how God is love; therefore, every time we see the word *love* in the text we can replace it with *God.* So we read it again saying, "God is patient; God is kind. . . ." Then we discussed being made in God's image. If we are created in God's image and aspire to be like Christ, essentially we are to live in such a way that we could replace *love* in the scripture with our own name: For example, "Ciona is patient; Ciona is kind. . . ."

This fascinated me! Personalizing this text created in me a deep need to repent, and it gave me a vision. I knew that my name did not belong with those words because I am not always patient or kind. But it became a visionary prayer that I might aspire to be more like Christ, who is patient and kind, rejoicing in truth and hoping in all things.

Yes, the Bible was written to specific people at a specific time, and understanding the context improves our interpretation of the Bible. Yet the beauty of this ancient story is that it still speaks to us personally today.

The books of the Prophets (Isaiah through Malachi with the exception of Lamentations) are a great place to personalize the text. For example, Isaiah 43:1-3 becomes a direct promise to the reader: "(*Your name*), do not fear, for I have redeemed you; I have called you by name; you are mine. (*Your name*), when you pass through the waters, I will be with you."

We can also hear Jesus talk directly to us by personalizing some of the Gospel passages. For example, hear your name in Matthew 11:28-29: "Come to me, *Jason,* who is weary and burdened, and I will give you rest." "Take my yoke upon you, *Erica,* and learn from me; for I am gentle and humble in heart, and you will find rest for your soul."

WRITING PSALMS

Day 5 Exercise

READ PSALM 136:1-9, 23-26.

> *O give thanks to the L*ORD*, for he is good,*
> *for his steadfast love endures forever.*
> —Psalm 136:1

REFLECT Practice rewriting this psalm or write one of your own. You might wish to write your own psalm as an acrostic in which each line starts with the next letter of the alphabet (you can choose any portion of alphabet):

A *Alleluia* to God, who gives me life.

B *Believe* what Jesus told me is the way to live.

C *Compassion* and justice are the way for me.

D *Devotion* to God is what I need for this

E *even* though I don't always feel like it.

PRAY Pray your psalm aloud. Start softly, whispering your prayer to God. Then read with a louder voice. Read with confidence that God hears and holds your personal prayer.

ACT View your world today through gratefulness for God's steadfast love.

Day 5 Reading

The psalmists opened themselves to God, exposing their fears, joys, pleas, hopes, and praise. Their words are lyrical, honest conversations with God. We all have psalms within us.

The book of Psalms is written in Hebrew poetic style, which does not have to rhyme. This style uses strong imagery and repetition. The Psalms are sprinkled with metaphors, such as "they are like trees planted by streams of water" (Ps. 1:3). Psalms also include personification, giving human characteristics to nature: "the heavens are telling the glory of God" (Ps. 19:1). Phrases like "his steadfast love endures forever" (Ps. 136) may be repeated in the manner of song refrains. Some Hebrew poems took the form of acrostics, in which every line or section started with a different letter of the Hebrew alphabet.

The Psalms have many different themes. There are songs and prayers for deliverance from enemies, healing from illness, and protection. The Psalms also express thanksgiving and praise, awe at creation, faith in the law, and confidence in God's power. When writing our own psalms, we can keep in mind the imagery of Hebrew poetry and approach our writing with styles we may know better.

Free verse without any poetic form works well. Consider rhyming a psalm. Here are examples of other poetry forms that are fun to try as well:

Haiku
Line 1: five syllables; Line 2: seven syllables; Line 3: five syllables

You smooth my edges
Like water over a rock
Your love covers me

Acrostic
Choose an idea or name and write it down the edge of your paper. Create a poem by starting each line with a word using these initial letters.

Forgive my tears; they keep falling.
Even though I want to trust you, fright
Attacks like a lion on the prowl.
Rescue me, Lord!

NOTES

WEEK TWO

1. Abraham Joshua Heschel, *God in Search of Man: A Philosophy of Judaism* (New York: Farrar, Straus and Giroux, 1955), 25.

2. Martha Graybeal Rowlett, *In Spirit and in Truth* (Nashville: Upper Room Books, 1982), 88.

WEEK THREE

1. John Wesley, "A Letter to Mr. Jonathan Maskew," quoted in Rueben P. Job and Norman Shawchuck, *A Guide to Prayer for All Who Seek God* (Nashville: Upper Room Books, 2003), 138.

WEEK FOUR

1. Heschel, *God in Search of Man*, 252.

2. Thomas à Kempis, *The Imitation of Christ*, rev. ed. by Joseph N. Tylenda (New York: Vintage Books, 1998), 49.

3. Based on "Meditating on the Word" in *Companions in Christ: A Small-Group Experience in Spiritual Formation* Participant's Book (Nashville: Upper Room Books, 2001), 84.

WEEK SIX

1. Mark Yaconelli, *Contemplative Youth Ministry: Practicing the Presence of Jesus* (Grand Rapids, Mich.: Zondervan Youth Specialties, 2006), 171–72.

2. Dietrich Bonhoeffer, *Meditating on the Word*, trans. David Gracie (Boston: Cowley Publications, 1986), 117.

JOURNAL PAGE

JOURNAL PAGE

JOURNAL PAGE

JOURNAL PAGE

JOURNAL PAGE

JOURNAL PAGE

JOURNAL PAGE

JOURNAL PAGE